THE BRAIN WORKS

X-TRAIN YOUR BRAIN

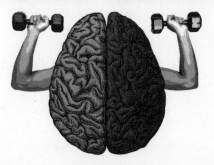

LEVEL 2: BUILDING CORE STRENGTH

PUTTING YOUR LEFT AND RIGHT BRAIN TO THE TEST TO ENHANCE ALERTNESS AND MENTAL AGILITY

CORINNE L. GEDIMAN WITH FRANCIS M. CRINELLA, PH.D.

DEDICATION

To the memory of Harry Lille
— *Corinne L. Gediman*

Published by Sellers Publishing, Inc.
Copyright © 2012 Sellers Publishing Inc.
Text and puzzles copyright © 2012 Corinne L. Gediman
All rights reserved.

Sellers Publishing, Inc.
161 John Roberts Road, South Portland, Maine 04106
Visit our Web site: www.sellerspublishing.com
E-mail: rsp@rsvp.com

ISBN 13: 978-1-4162-0853-2

Designed by George Corsillo/Design Monsters

10 9 8 7 6 5 4 3 2 1

Printed and bound in the United States of America.

CONTENTS

LEVEL 2: BUILDING CORE STRENGTH

The goal of *The Brain Works: X-Train Your Brain* series is to get your brain back to peak performance by rejuvenating specific mental functions before serious decline sets in. It is much easier to maintain mental abilities than to try to regain them, in the same way that it is easier to maintain muscle tone than to try to regain it. A successful exercise program needs to be comprehensive, confidence building, and fun. *The Brain Works: X-Train Your Brain* series is designed to meet all three of these criteria.

Level 2 is the second in a series of brain-exercise workout books designed to help you build a better brain. The exercises are fun and engaging, and success is easy. This is the "core strength" phase of your brain-exercise program. As you advance through the exercise levels, you will build increased brain stamina and resilience. Each level brings you closer to a brighter and healthier brain. If you did the puzzles in *X-Train Your Brain: Level 1: Basic Warm-Up*, it is not necessary to read the rest of the Introduction again. However, even if you took the Brain-Dominance Self-Assesment in Level 1, you may want to take it again to confirm your initial assessment of your right- or left-brain dominance. If you did not do the puzzles in the first book, it is highly recommended that you read the following, which provides the rationale and framework for your brain-fitness workout.

As in Level 1, the exercises are a mix of left brain (verbal), right brain (visual, spatial), and whole brain (right-left intuitive thinking). You will see some familiar exercise formats, as well as many new exercise types. Now that your brain has woken up and warmed up, you are ready for new brain challenges at a slightly higher level of mental stretching. Remember, the key to brain fitness is to keep presenting your brain with new experiences.

USE IT OR LOSE IT!

Whether you are a busy professional, a multitasking soccer mom, or a retiree, your quality of life depends on the health and resilience of your brain. Using new brain-imaging technology, neuroscientists can see that brain aging begins in our early twenties, and that memory peaks at around age thirty. While this is disturbing news, there is a bright side, and our fate is not sealed.

The last decade has brought a wealth of knowledge about the brain and how it works. Perhaps the most amazing revelation is the brain's miraculous regenerative powers, known as neural plasticity. While once it was believed that brain aging was inevitable, it is now certain that exercising your brain by presenting it with novelty and mental challenges can help ward off mental decline and result in a brighter and healthier brain throughout your lifetime.

Without mental stimulation, however, brain cells slowly atrophy and die, much like body muscles that go unused. When presented with mental challenges, brain cells light up and axons (nerve fibers) start firing. This electrical-chemical activity gets brain cells "talking" to each other. It is this "chatter" that leads to new communication pathways and stronger neuronal connections between brain cells. The result is a healthier, more resilient brain capable of delaying and even warding off dementia and other diseases of the brain. And the best part is that building a brawnier brain is a lifestyle choice.

EXERCISE FOR A BETTER BRAIN

X-Train Your Brain is a brain-exercise program designed by experts in the field. It works on the proven principle that mental muscle, much like physical muscle, can be gained and maintained through an exercise regimen. The program parallels a physical workout routine at your gym, in which you begin by warming up unused muscles, progress to building core strength, and then increase your stamina and accelerate the pace.

There are four exercise levels contained in this series. Each level builds on the last and brings you closer to a better brain.

  Level 1: Basic Warm-Up (Stress Free)
  Level 2: Building Core Strength (Easy)
  Level 3: Increasing Stamina (Moderate)
  Level 4: Accelerating the Pace (More Challenging)

X-TRAIN EXERCISE GOAL

Just as a sedentary lifestyle won't keep your body in peak physical condition, a sedentary brain won't retain its mental edge. Retaining peak mental performance is the key to reversing the mental deficits associated with an aging brain, including memory loss, sluggish thinking, and problem-solving confusion.

COMPREHENSIVE

Athletes achieve peak physical performance through cross-training, and we apply this same method for brain athletes. Cross-training your brain makes perfect sense, given the brain's own natural anatomy. The two hemispheres of the cerebral cortex (gray matter) are divided right down the middle into a left hemisphere and a right hemisphere. Each side of the brain is specialized and shows dominance with regard to specific mental processes and abilities. The "left brain" excels at verbal abilities, logic, and linear problem solving, while the "right brain" is adept at visual perception, spatial relationships, and creative problem solving. Collectively these abilities contribute to a fully functioning whole brain. *X-Train Your Brain* targets both left- and right-brain functions and mental abilities, for a comprehensive and total-brain workout.

CONFIDENCE BUILDING

X-Train Your Brain is designed to build confidence and demonstrate your gains. At the gym, progress is easy to see. While last month I was lifting 5-pound weights, this month I can lift 10-pound weights. When I started my workout program, I was doing 15 minutes on the treadmill; now I'm doing 45 minutes.

Level 1 of this series starts off with exercises and games that are fun and easily mastered. This ensures a satisfying, no-stress experience, allowing you to increase your mental stamina at a comfortable, relaxed pace. As you move forward you'll gain the confidence and skills to take on greater challenges. To facilitate success, all of the exercises are preceded by "how to" instructions and examples, so that you know exactly how to approach each puzzle or game.

FUN

Sticking with an exercise program is not easy, as evidenced by lapsed gym memberships and retired exercise equipment sitting in basements. Despite good intentions, physical exercise can become routine, time-consuming, and somewhat boring. That's why only highly motivated, type A personalities tend to stick with it over time.

It's essential to avoid these same pitfalls in a brain-exercise program. The *X-Train Your Brain* series is anything but routine, boring, or time-consuming. Every exercise brings novelty and a new, intriguing mental challenge. Exercises are structured as games and puzzles to ensure a fun and enjoyable workout. And you set your own pace. Success isn't determined by how many exercises you do in a sitting, or how many you get right. Success means bringing some mental challenge and novelty to your brain every day to keep it sharp and agile. The goal is a better quality of mental life.

Since many of the exercises are set up like games, they can be enjoyed by more than one person, or even by competing teams. To turn an exercise into a friendly game, simply add a time limit by which it has to be completed. The winner is the player or team that generates the most responses in a given time frame. Adding timed play to the challenge helps you work on your mental-processing speed, which slows down with age.

BRAIN DOMINANCE

Before you get started, it's interesting to know which side of your brain is dominant. Brain dominance relates to specific mental functions and thinking styles. Most people have a preferred brain-dominance orientation. Your brain dominance will create an affinity for and ease with some puzzles over others. If you are left-brain dominant, you'll definitely enjoy the word games but may struggle with the visual puzzles, and vice versa. You may even be tempted to stick with the exercises that match your brain dominance and skip those that do not. But that would defeat the purpose of a cross-training program, and your gains would be minimized. Remember, the more a mental workout takes you out of your comfort zone, the more novelty it brings to your brain. And the greatest gains come with novelty, because new brain pathways are being tapped.

LEFT-BRAIN CHARACTERISTICS

The left side of the brain excels at language skills, verbal processing, sequential reasoning, and analytical thinking. Individuals who favor this type of thinking are said to be left-brain dominant. They are characterized as logical and rational thinkers capable of excelling in many fields, including science, mathematics, writing, accounting, financial services, teaching, medicine, engineering, research, library science, and computer programming. When problem solving, left-brain-dominant thinkers arrive at the solution or big picture by analyzing and organizing the step-by-step details along the way. They are good forward planners and usually enjoy "talking out" a problem. This brain orientation is compatible with traditional classroom learning, in which students are rewarded for finding the "right" answer.

RIGHT-BRAIN CHARACTERISTICS

The right side of the brain shows dominance in visual-spatial reasoning, random processing (i.e., free association), intuition, perceptual organization, and holistic thinking. Holistic thinkers are able to "see" the "whole" as a picture. They retain information through the use of images and patterns. Perceptual organization, a right-brain-dominant strength, is the process by which the brain takes bits and pieces of visual information (color, lines, shapes) and structures the individual parts into larger units and interrelationships. Individuals who excel in perceptual organization show an ability to arrange color, lines, and shapes into creative works of art, sculpture, and architecture. In school, right-brain-dominant children are whizzes at solving visual challenges, such as puzzles, mazes, block building, hidden blocks, and visual mathematical patterns. In fact, they may be brilliant mathematicians who easily grasp geometry and physics, but be poor calculators who struggle to grasp the linear logic in algebra. Some occupations that attract a right-brain person are inventor, architect, forest ranger, illustrator, artist, actor, athlete, interior decorator, beautician, mathematician, computer-graphics designer, craftsperson, photographer, recreation director, marketing designer, retail specialist, yoga/dance instructor, art director, Web-site designer, fashion designer, and product-package designer.

The Brain-Dominance Self-Assessment below will provide insight into whether you are naturally left-brain or right-brain dominant. It will help you understand where your mental strengths lie, as well as what your greatest "mental stretch" opportunities are.

For each item, circle the letter "a" or "b" beside the answer that most closely describes your preference. You must choose either "a" or "b" — you cannot choose both. If you are not sure, consider what your response would be if you were in a stressful, difficult, or new situation. We tend to revert to our natural brain dominance when under pressure.

1 Do you often find yourself following your hunches?
   a. yes
   b. no

2 When you are learning dance steps, it is easier for you to . . .
   a. learn by imitation and by getting the feel of the music.
   b. learn the sequence of movements and talk yourself through it.

3 Do you like to rearrange your furniture several times a year?
   a. yes
   b. no

4 Can you tell approximately how much time has passed without a watch?
   a. yes
   b. no

5 In school, was it easier for you to understand algebra or geometry?
   a. algebra
   b. geometry

6 Do you think logically most of the time about why people behave in a certain manner?
   a. yes
   b. no

7 When given a topic in school, would you prefer to express your feelings through drawing or writing?
   a. drawing
   b. writing

8 When someone is talking to you, do you respond to the content of what is said (word meaning), or to how it is said (feelings, voice pitch)?
   a. what is said
   b. how it is said

9 Is it easier for you to read for the main ideas or to read for specific details?
    a. main ideas
    b. specific details

10 Do you feel more comfortable saying/doing humorous things or saying/doing well-reasoned things?
    a. humorous things
    b. well-reasoned things

11 Are you interested in psychology and holistic healing?
    a. yes
    b. no

12 Do many people think your workspace is messy?
    a. yes
    b. no

13 Do you sometimes act spontaneously or come to premature conclusions?
    a. yes
    b. no

14 Can you always find the right word to describe your feelings?
    a. yes
    b. no

15 Are you objective in your opinions, weighing the facts carefully?
    a. yes
    b. no

16 Are a romantic dreamer or a logical planner?
    a. romantic dreamer
    b. logical planner

17 Are you interested in science and technology?
    a. yes
    b. no

18 If you had to choose, would you rather attend a lecture or go to an artistic event (dance performance, concert, art exhibit)?

      a. lecture
      b. artistic event

19 Do you have the patience to approach a task from different angles until you find a solution?

      a. yes
      b. no

20 Do you like puzzles and word games?

      a. yes
      b. no

21 If you forget someone's name, would you go through the alphabet until you remembered it?

      a. yes
      b. no

22 Have you considered being a poet, a politician, an architect, or a dancer?

      a. yes
      b. no

23 Have you considered becoming a lawyer, a journalist, or a doctor?

      a. yes
      b. no

24 Do you enjoy learning a foreign language?

      a. yes
      b. no

25 Is it easy for you to categorize and put away files?

      a. yes
      b. no

Brain-Dominance Answer Key

If your answers to the questions above are fairly evenly distributed between left- and right-brain responses, you are a "whole brain" thinker with the flexibility to draw on the strengths of both brain hemispheres. If the majority of your responses fall into one or the other brain-hemisphere categories, your natural tendencies are to draw on the strengths of your primary brain dominance as you engage in everyday activities and challenges.

Left-Brain Responses: 1. b, 2. b, 3. b, 4. a, 5. a, 6. a, 7. b, 8. a, 9. b, 10. b, 11. b, 12. b, 13. b, 14. a, 15. a, 16. b, 17. a, 18. a, 19. a, 20. a, 21. a, 22. b, 23. a, 24. a, 25. a

Right-Brain Responses: 1. a, 2. a, 3. a, 4. b, 5. b, 6. b, 7. a, 8. b, 9. a, 10. a, 11. a, 12. a, 13. a, 14. b, 15. b, 16. a, 17. b, 18. b, 19. b, 20. b, 21. b, 22. a, 23. b, 24. b, 25. b

You are now ready to begin your journey toward becoming a brain athlete! Remember that the key is to relax and have fun. Did you know that stress kills brain cells? So no stressing. You are about to do something really good for yourself. Enjoy it and feel proud.

PART 1:
LEFT BRAIN

Can You Say It?

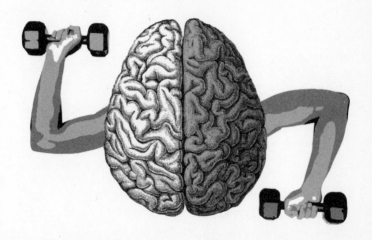

Verbal Exercises

LEFT BRAIN: CAN YOU SAY IT? VERBAL EXERCISES

INTRODUCTION:

The focus of the left-brain exercises is on the left hemisphere's natural proclivity for language skills. Keeping language processing sharp as we age is critical to memory formation, storage, and retrieval. In this left-brain workout, you will participate in a variety of entertaining verbal exercises.

LEFT   RIGHT

Logic
Analysis
Sequencing
Linear Reasoning
Mathematics
Language
Facts
Thinking in Words
Words of Songs
Computation

HOW TO PLAY:

Heteronyms are words that are spelled the same but differ in meaning and pronunciation (e.g., *bow* down to the king; shoot the arrow with the *bow*). In this game, you will be given an original sentence containing a heteronym. Your brain challenge is to look at the heteronym (in italics) in each sentence and provide the alternative definition for the word in the space below. Suppose the original sentence is "Jane, please *close* the door on your way out." Since "close" (meaning "shut") is the heteronym, then your answer would be as follows:

Alternative definition of heteronym: *to stand nearby*

SET ONE:
AT WORK

1. The computer *console* is taking up too much space on my desk.

   Alternative definition of heteronym: _____

2. The in-focus machine *projects* the image from your computer onto the screen.

   Alternative definition of heteronym: _____

3. Her boss told her that her *conduct* in the meeting was unacceptable.

   Alternative definition of heteronym: _____

4. The college student was hired as an *intern* for the summer.

   Alternative definition of heteronym: _____

5. The interviewer was impressed with her business *resume*.

   Alternative definition of heteronym: _____

ANSWER KEY

HETERONYMS

Set One: At Work

1. comfort
2. plans
3. lead
4. confine
5. start over

HOW TO PLAY:
See instructions on page 15.

SET TWO:
LEGAL EAGLE

1. I always *refuse* to sign a document I have not read.

   Alternative definition of heteronym: _____

2. It's hard for a team to *digest* the loss of a talented player.

   Alternative definition of heteronym: _____

3. Please *relay* the message to the judge.

   Alternative definition of heteronym: _____

4. The lawyer will file an appeal and *contest* the verdict.

   Alternative definition of heteronym: _____

5. The accountant must not *overlook* important data when testifying about financial fraud.

   Alternative definition of heteronym: _____

ANSWER KEY

HETERONYMS

Set Two: Legal Eagle

1. garbage
2. a condensed version
3. race
4. competition
5. elevated spot with a view

HOW TO PLAY:
See instructions on page 15.

SET THREE:
MUSIC & ARTS

1. She plays the *bass* cello in the orchestra.

   Alternative definition of heteronym: _____

2. The singer was asked to *moderate* the vibrato in her voice.

   Alternative definition of heteronym: _____

3. The actress made her *entrance* stage left.

   Alternative definition of heteronym: _____

4. She was assigned to an *intermediate*-level dance class.

   Alternative definition of heteronym: _____

5. The performance made the audience *tear* up.

   Alternative definition of heteronym: _____

ANSWER KEY

HETERONYMS

Set Three: Music & Arts

1. fish
2. middle-of-the-roader
3. put in a trance
4. intervene
5. cry

HETERONYMS

HOW TO PLAY:
See instructions on page 15.

SET FOUR:
WIND & WATER

1. The water started seeping in, as the retaining wall began to *degenerate*.

   Alternative definition of heteronym: _____

2. The hurricane-force *wind* blew off the roof tiles.

   Alternative definition of heteronym: _____

3. The rain went down the *sewer* drain.

   Alternative definition of heteronym: _____

4. The rope on the boat was *wound* into tight coils.

   Alternative definition of heteronym: _____

5. The sailor *dove* into the sea to cool off.

   Alternative definition of heteronym: _____

ANSWER KEY

HETERONYMS

Set Four: Wind & Water

1. a lowlife
2. coil
3. one who sews
4. injury
5. a bird

HOW TO PLAY:
See instructions on page 15.

SET FIVE:
PLAY BALL

1. The referee called it an *invalid* play.

   Alternative definition of heteronym: _____

2. He rarely got to play in the game, because he was an *alternate* player.

   Alternative definition of heteronym: _____

3. A good coach will *produce* a winning team.

   Alternative definition of heteronym: _____

4. The quarterback will take the *lead* in a football game.

   Alternative definition of heteronym: _____

5. The bleachers got a coat of white *primer*.

   Alternative definition of heteronym: _____

ANSWER KEY

HETERONYMS

Set Five: Play Ball

1. one who is sickly
2. to switch back and forth
3. fruits & vegetables
4. toxic metal
5. first learning book

AUTO-ANTONYMS

HOW TO PLAY

Auto-antonyms are a type of heteronym. Auto-antonyms are words that sound the same, but have opposite meanings. For example, the word "root" means "to firmly establish" (e.g., to put down roots). "Root" also means "to remove" (e.g., to root out crime in our community). As in the prior game, you will be given an original sentence containing an auto-antonym. Your brain challenge is to look at the auto-antonyms (in italics) in each sentence and provide the alternative definition for the word in the space below.

SET ONE:
AROUND THE HOUSE

1. The electric *bill* must be paid.
   Alternative definition of auto-antonym: _____

2. The lock was secured with a *bolt*.
   Alternative definition of auto-antonym: _____

3. At her desk, she kept rubber bands to *clip* letters together.
   Alternative definition of auto-antonym: _____

4. He always *left* the house key under the mat.
   Alternative definition of auto-antonym: _____

5. After a number of robberies, the neighbors decided to form a community *oversight* committee to look into the matter.
   Alternative definition of auto-antonym: _____

6. Before the guests arrived, she needed to *dust* the furniture in the guest bedroom.
   Alternative definition of auto-antonym: _____

7. Despite the gale-force wind and rain, the house was able to *weather* the storm.
   Alternative definition of auto-antonym: _____

ANSWER KEY

AUTO-ANTONYMS

Set One: Around the House

1. currency
2. dash away
3. cut off
4. exited
5. omission
6. sprinkle with fine particles
7. wear away

HOW TO PLAY:

See instructions on page 25. Note, for Set two your brain challenge is to identify the auto-antonym in each sentence and provide the alternative definition for the word in the space below.

SET TWO:
MIXED BAG

1. The patient said to the nurse, "Please help me buckle my belt."

   Alternative definition of auto-antonym: _____

2. It is the custom of the country to bow to the king and queen.

   Alternative definition of auto-antonym: _____

3. Her broken wrist was a physical handicap that prevented her from playing golf.

   Alternative definition of auto-antonym: _____

4. She was easily impregnable and gave birth to 11 children in her lifetime.

   Alternative definition of auto-antonym: _____

5. Rather than go to the groomer, she trims the dog's toenails herself.

   Alternative definition of auto-antonym: _____

6. When he replaced the telephone receiver, the call was disconnected.

   Alternative definition of auto-antonym: _____

7. Her friends loved her for her upbeat and sanguine nature.

   Alternative definition of auto-antonym: _____

Answer Key

AUTO-ANTONYMS

Set Two: Mixed Bag

1. buckle; collapse

2. custom; specialized, unique

3. handicap; advantage (golf)

4. impregnable; impossible to enter

5. trims; adds (ornament)

6. receiver; one who receives or is awarded something

7. sanguine; murderous

HOW TO PLAY:

Homonyms are often used to create a witty "play on words," (e.g., there's a rabbit breeder who combs his *hare* every morning). They are words that sound exactly or almost exactly the same, have different meanings, and are spelled differently. You will be presented with a sentence that is missing two words. Fill in the blanks with the two homonyms that will make a logical sentence. For example, *It's a ____ idea to try to ____ yourself a glass of milk with your eyes closed.* The two homonyms that would make a sensible sentence are *poor* and *pour*.

SET ONE:
COLORFUL PHRASES

1. My father recently _____ *The Hunt for* _____ *October.*

2. The toy boat with the red _____ was on _____.

3. When I spilled the cake _____, every _____ in the vase turned white.

4. I _____ out my birthday candles, even though it made me _____ in the face.

5. The _____ _____ a mistake and cleaned the coffee table with brown shoe polish.

ANSWER KEY

HOMONYMS

Set One: Colorful Phrases

1. read, *Red*
2. sail, sale
3. flour, flower
4. blew, blue
5. maid, made

HOW TO PLAY:

See instructions on page 29.

SET TWO:
ACTION PHRASES

1. It takes a _____ lot of time and sweat to dig a deep _____.

2. It's easy to fall off a _____ if you _____ straight ahead instead of down.

3. He tried to _____ the fly with an old _____.

4. I _____ my bike all day on a country _____, and now my legs are sore.

5. It's not _____ easy to _____ your own clothes.

ANSWER KEY

HOMONYMS

Set Two: Action Phrases

1. whole, hole
2. stair, stare
3. shoo, shoe
4. rode, road
5. so, sew

HOW TO PLAY:
See instructions on page 29.

SET THREE:
FOOD PHRASES

1. _____ could use a _____ bit more bread and butter on our table.

2. When my older sister was slicing a _____, she told me that the distance around it is _____ times the distance across it.

3. I think the dog went to _____ his bone under the _____ tree.

4. I would not _____ to sit next to someone who _____ his food loudly.

5. The food they serve on a _____ tastes very _____.

ANSWER KEY

HOMONYMS

Set Three: Food Phrases

1. We, wee
2. pie, pi
3. bury, berry
4. choose, chews
5. plane, plain

HOW TO PLAY:
See instructions on page 29.

SET FOUR:
FACTUAL PHRASES

1. A torn Achilles _____ can take a long time to _____.

2. The producers of *Bambi* made a lot of _____ from a little fawn and a white-tailed _____.

3. You can usually _____ many more stars in the night sky when you're high above _____ level.

4. Many years ago, _____ were allowed to work as coal _____.

5. You're not allowed to _____ products for money if you are in a prison _____.

ANSWER KEY

HOMONYMS

Set Four: Factual Phrases

1. heel, heal
2. dough, doe
3. see, sea
4. minors, miners
5. sell, cell

HOW TO PLAY:
See instructions on page 29.

SET FIVE:
KID PHRASES

1. The little kid playing with the _____ and shovel has a very _____ complexion.

2. My teacher's _____ has sensitive skin and can't stay out in the _____ too long.

3. _____ kids stayed at the fair for one _____.

4. My kid _____ the test because he knew about the _____ presidents of the twentieth century.

5. The kids' _____ was _____ from playing in places where you have to be at least 21.

ANSWER KEY

HOMONYMS

Set Five: Kid Phrases

1. pail, pale
2. son, sun
3. Our, hour
4. passed, past
5. band, banned

HOW TO PLAY:
See instructions on page 29.

SET SIX:
POTPOURRI

1. The story about a lizard with a fifty-foot _____ is nothing but a tall _____.

2. I _____ that _____ was spelled with a silent g.

3. So far, my team has _____ _____ more game than your team.

4. It _____ be fun to be able to make a _____ carving.

5. I _____ with my _____ hand.

ANSWER KEY

HOMONYMS

Set Six: Potpourri

1. tail, tale
2. knew, gnu
3. won, one
4. would, wood
5. write, right

HOW TO PLAY

Certain consonants, like l and r, are in many words, and other consonants are in much fewer words. Maybe because they're pretty rare, words with x, j, and k seem to have funny and memorable sounds. It's hard not to love words like "foxy" and "kooky." In this series of games, each of these crazy consonants takes a turn starring in two different words or names in a sentence. You get to see where the crazy consonant appears (sometimes more than once in the same word) and how many letters come before and after it. The trick is to find both words or names with the crazy consonant so that the sentence makes sense.

SET ONE:
LOVE THAT X

1. If you ___ ___ ___ ___x your grip on the __ x, it may go flying out of your hand.

2. A ___ ___ x ___ ___ ___ ___ has ___ ___ x sides.

3. The weight lifter thought he could lift a little ___ x ___ ___ ___ weight, if he would ___ ___ ___ x his muscles before lifting.

4. The technician was trying to ___ ___ x the x-___ ___ ___ machine.

5. If you ___ ___ x shoe polish with floor ___ ___ x, you'll have a messy floor.

6. Dad says he pays enough income ___ ___ x to buy all the gold in Fort ___ ___ ___ x.

7. There's a new ___ ___ x of Wheat ___ ___ ___ x in the pantry.

8. The Rio Grande goes through both ___ ___ x ___ ___ and New ___ ___ x ___ ___ ___.

9. Richard ___ ___ x ___ ___ was first elected president in nineteen-hundred ___ ___ x ___ ___ -eight.

10. If Tinker Bell lived in Alabama, some people might have called her a ___ ___ x ___ ___ from ___ ___ x ___ ___.

ANSWER KEY

CRAZY CONSONANTS: X, J & K

Set One: Love That X

1. relax, ax
2. hexagon, six
3. extra, flex
4. fix, x-ray
5. mix, wax
6. tax, Knox
7. box, Chex
8. Texas, Mexico
9. Nixon, sixty
10. pixie, Dixie

HOW TO PLAY:

In this puzzle, you must find the last name of a famous film star hidden in a sentence about him or her. Here is an example:

"He stood _ TALL_ _ _ when he played Rocky Balboa."

Who is the famous actor hidden in the sentence?

Add letters to form a name. That's right — Sylvester Stallone.

WHAT IS THE NAME OF THE ACTOR HIDDEN IN EACH SENTENCE?

1. He played a B _ A _ D_ guy in *The Godfather*.

2. Her fans went to S _ _ EE _ her in *Julie & Julia*.

3. He owned a B _ _ A R _ in *Casablanca*.

4. He had a famous movie _ C _ _ A R _ E _ E _ _ _ R before he became a state governor.

5. The hills A _ _ R E _ _ alive with the sound of her music.

6. He _ _ C _ _ A N claim credit for the evil character of Lex Luthor in the *Superman* films.

7. The ladies swoon when watching this sexy dance star S W A Y _ _ to the music in films like *Dirty Dancing*.

8. She _ _ R A N _ _ _ away with her best friend in the movie *Thelma and Louise*.

9. This movie star appeared in _ O N _ _ *Golden Pond* with his real-life daughter.

10. This glamorous blonde actress was _ O N _ _ _ President Kennedy's top-ten guest list while he was in the White House.

ANSWER KEY

FILM STARS

What Is the Name of the Actor Hidden in Each Sentence?

1. Brando
2. Streep
3. Bogart
4. Schwarzenegger
5. Andrews
6. Hackman
7. Swayze
8. Sarandon
9. Fonda
10. Monroe

HOW TO PLAY:

In this game, you will be given five sets of scrambled words. Each of the scrambled words belongs to a specific category. One word, however, does not fit the category. It is a pretender. Unscramble the words to find the pretender. You will be given the pretender category as a clue.

SET ONE: FLOWERS
PRETENDER CATEGORY: SCHOOL SUPPLY

Scrambled	Unscrambled
ADIFDLOF	
TEVLOI	
LIGAMROD	
IYDSA	
NCLIPE	

ANSWER KEY

CATEGORY SCRAMBLER

Set One:

Flowers: daffodil, violet, marigold, daisy

Pretender: *pencil*

CATEGORY SCRAMBLER

HOW TO PLAY:
See instructions on page 45.

SET TWO: MUSICAL INSTRUMENTS
PRETENDER CATEGORY: WEDDING ACCESSORY

Scrambled	Unscrambled
BMONRTOE	
RSHOAIDPCR	
UQEBUOT	
COOLIPC	
TIRGAU	

ANSWER KEY

CATEGORY SCRAMBLER

Set Two:

Musical Instruments: trombone, harpsichord, piccolo, guitar,

Pretender: *bouquet*

Category Scrambler

How to Play:
See instructions on page 45.

Set Three: Beach Sights
Pretender Category: Movie Food

Scrambled	Unscrambled
OPRNOPC	
RUSERF	
SMWMIRE	
RBELUAML	
ASND	

ANSWER KEY

CATEGORY SCRAMBLER

Set Three:

Beach Sights: surfer, swimmer, umbrella, sand

Pretender: *popcorn*

CATEGORY SCRAMBLER

HOW TO PLAY:
See instructions on page 45.

SET FOUR: TYPES OF FISH
PRETENDER CATEGORY: FOOTWEAR

Scrambled	Unscrambled
SNAMLO	
ACREEKML	
NESAREKS	
PRCEH	
SBSA	

ANSWER KEY

CATEGORY SCRAMBLER

Set Four:

Types of Fish: salmon, mackerel, perch, bass

Pretender: *sneakers*

CATEGORY SCRAMBLER

HOW TO PLAY:
See instructions on page 45.

SET FIVE: MIDDLE-EASTERN COUNTRIES
PRETENDER CATEGORY: EUROPEAN COUNTRY

Scrambled	Unscrambled
AYRSI	
LRIESA	
PTGYE	
CNRFAE	
KUTAWI	

ANSWER KEY

CATEGORY SCRAMBLER

Set Five:

Middle-Eastern Countries: Syria, Israel, Egypt, Kuwait

Pretender: *France*

How to Play:

In this game, you will be presented with five sets of matrixes filled with letters. The objective is to form words by connecting adjacent letters. Letters that are above, below, to the left or right, or on a diagonal to each other are all acceptable connections. For each set, you will be given one free word clue. See how quickly you can find the free word. Play against a friend to see who can find the most words. Or see how many words you can find in two minutes.

Set One:

Free Word Clue: What happens when your car breaks down on the road?

C	R	U	L
A	K	P	S
G	T	W	E
B	O	H	D

Free Word-Clue Answer:

Other Words:

ANSWER KEY

WORD BOGGLER

Set One:

Free Word Clue: What happens when your car breaks down on the road?

Free Word-Clue Answer: towed

Other words:

six letters: slurped, pulsed, carped, tarps, swept

five letters: slurp, pulse, depth, carps

four letters: wept, used, tows, toga, tarp, tack, swot, swob, spur, spew, sped, slur, ruse, rack plus, pews, owed, lurk, hews, carp, bows, both

three letters: who, wed, use, ups, two, tow, tog, the, tar, tag, sew, rat, rag, pus, pew, owe, how, hot, hog, got, dew, cat, car, bow, bog, ark arc, ago

See instructions on page 55.

Set Two:

Free Word Clue: What keeps cold hands warm?

C	A	N	T
L	K	P	B
G	O	E	T
B	M	V	S

Free Word-Clue Answer:

Other Words:

ANSWER KEY

WORD BOGGLER

Set Two:

Free Word Clue: What keeps cold hands warm?

Free Word-Clue Answer: gloves

Other words:

six to seven letters: packets, packet, cloves

five letters: polka, pokes, poets, napes, moves, loves, glove, clove, clank, capes, cakes,

four letters: vets, step, stem, poke, poet, poem, pets, pest, pant, pack, opts, opal, move, mope, love, lope, lake, lack, kept, goes, glob, clog, clap, clan, cape, calk, cake, bets, best, apes, aloe

three letters: vet, set, pet, pan, pal, opt, nap, mop, mob, lop, log, lob, lap, cap, can, bog, bet, apt, ape, ant

HOW TO PLAY:
See instructions on page 55.

SET THREE:
FREE WORD CLUE: WHAT DO FLOWERS NEED?

P	G	A	D
E	R	O	R
I	T	W	A
B	H	A	S

FREE WORD-CLUE ANSWER:

OTHER WORDS:

ANSWER KEY

WORD BOGGLER

Set Three:

Free Word Clue: What do flowers need?

Free Word-Clue Answer: water

Other words:

six letters: whiter, toward, satire, regard, growth

five letters: wrote, write, worth, white, water, thaws, swore, sword, swath, hater, grows, draws, biter, birth, award, aorta, adore

four letters: wore, word, what, ward, trod, tows, tore, toad, tire, thaw, swat, rows, rote, roar, road, rite, rare, rage, prow, prod, ogre, hire, hate, grow, grit, gore, goad, ergo, draw, drag, dart, bite

three letters: was, war, two, tow, tie, saw, sat, row, rot, rod, rib, raw, rag, pet, peg, ore, oar, ire, hit, hat, has, got, god, get, ego, dot, dog, bit, ate, are, ago, age

HOW TO PLAY:
See instructions on page 55.

SET FOUR:
FREE WORD CLUE: WHERE DO YOU SIT IN A GYM?

V	P	O	B
E	R	L	E
S	H	A	T
K	C	W	I

FREE WORD-CLUE ANSWER:

OTHER WORDS:

ANSWER KEY

WORD BOGGLER

Set Four:

Free Word Clue: Where do you sit in a gym?

Free Word-Clue Answer: bleachers

Other words:

six to seven letters: kreplach, chlorate, bleacher, teacher, scarlet, scalper, operate, whacks, eloper, chalet, bleach

five letters: whale, shack, teach, tacks, sharp, share, scare, scalp, scale, racks, probe, polar, pleat, plate, plait, lacks, hero, hacks, elope, carve, carol, bleat, blare, blahs, black, beach,

four letters: what, warp, ware, wait, tear, teal, tarp, tale, tack, scat, scar, rope, role, rate, rack, pore, poet, lore, lope, late, lack, hero, hate, harp, hare, halt, halo, hack, each, chat, carp, bolt, belt, beat, bear, aloe, ache

three letters: war, tea, tar, she, roe, rob, raw, rat, lop, lob, let, law, her, hat, era, eat, ear, caw, cat, car, bop, bet, ate, are, alp, ale

HOW TO PLAY:
See instructions on page 55.

SET FIVE:
FREE WORD CLUE: WHAT IS A TREAT YOU GET AT A BAKERY?

A	T	P	I
Y	E	U	N
R	W	P	B
A	T	S	A

FREE WORD-CLUE ANSWER:

OTHER WORDS:

ANSWER KEY

WORD BOGGLER

Set Five:

Free Word Clue: What is a treat you get at a bakery?

Free Word-Clue Answer: pastry

Other words:

six to seven letters: upswept, treaty, sweaty, repast, pinups, pastry,

five letters: warts, tubas, treat, swept, sweat, strep, straw, stare, pinup, pasta, input,

four letters: wept, wary, wart, ware, tubs, tuba, swat, star, spun, spew, rats, pups, pubs, pews, pert, peat, past, awry, arts, area, abut

three letters: yew, yet, yea, wry, wet, war, ups, tub, try, tea, tar, spa, sap, rye, raw, rat, put, pup, pun, pub, pin, pet, pep, pea, nut, nip, era, eat, but, bun, ate, asp, art, are, apt, ape

HOW TO PLAY:

In its simplest form, an analogy is a stated likeness between two things that are otherwise unlike. In solving an analogy, your first step is to determine the relationship between the first two italicized words. You must then select words for the second pairing that have a parallel relationship. In the example below, the relationship is about characteristics of each species:

A characteristic of a *bird* is its ability to *fly*, while a parallel characteristic of a *fish* its ability to *swim*.

Without putting pressure on yourself, time how long it takes you to complete Set One. Then try and beat your time in Set Two.

SET ONE:

TAKE IT EASY

1. *Dime* is to *ten* as *half* is to _____.

2. *Football* is to *helmet* as *soccer* is to _____.

3. *Rabbit* is to *hole* as *lion* is to _____.

4. *Down* is to *up* as *red* is to _____.

5. *Cell phone* is to *battery* as *television* is to _____.

6. *Road* is to *car* as *air* is to _____.

7. *Bring* is to *brought* as *go* is to _____.

8. *Conductor* is to *orchestra* as *coach* is to _____.

9. *Crab* is to *crustacean* as *mouse* is to _____.

10. *Seventy* is to *69* as *eight* is to _____.

ANSWER KEY

MIXED-UP ANALOGIES

Set One: Take It Easy

1. 50
2. shin guard
3. den
4. green
5. electricity
6. airplane
7. went
8. team
9. mammal
10. seven

HOW TO PLAY:
See instructions on page 65.

SET TWO:
PICK UP THE PACE

1. *Capital letter* is to *beginning* as *period* is to _____.

2. *Sunflower* is to *yellow* as *plum* is to _____.

3. *Pretty* is to *smile* as *ugly* is to _____.

4. *Touch* is to *feel* as *hear* is to _____.

5. *Crunch* is to *ice* as *slosh* is to _____.

6. *Walk* is to *slow* as *run* is to _____.

7. *Halloween* is to *witch* as *Thanksgiving* is to _____.

8. *Corn* is to *husk* as *peanut* is to _____.

9. *Joint* is to *orthopedic* as _____ is to *cardiac*.

10. *Window* is to *house* as _____ is to *face*.

ANSWER KEY

MIXED-UP ANALOGIES

Set Two: Pick Up the Pace

1. end
2. purple
3. frown
4. listen
5. water
6. fast
7. Pilgrim
8. shell
9. heart
10. eye

PREFIX FINDER

HOW TO PLAY:

An English word can consist of three parts: the *root*, a *prefix*, and a *suffix*. The root is the part of the word that contains its core meaning. Prefixes are attached to the beginning of a root word, and suffixes are attached to the end of the root word. Prefixes and suffixes change the word's meaning, as well as its use.

In this exercise, you will be presented with a list of words, all of which have a prefix. Your first task is to separate the root word from its prefix by drawing a line between them. Your second task is to fill in the spaces in the left-hand column with letters that correspond to the definitions in the right-hand column.

Here is an example: The word "react" can be divided into its prefix "re" and its root word "act" (re/act). Which of the following definitions matches the meaning of the prefix "re"? Is it *again, next,* or *before*? If you chose *again,* you made the right match. If you are not sure, try to think of other words with the same prefix, like "*re*bound." This will provide extra clues to the prefix's definition.

FIND THE PREFIX

1. transport _____
2. precede _____
3. circumference _____
4. midway _____
5. superintendent _____
6. defrost _____
7. polygamy _____
8. promote _____
9. subject _____
10. autobiography _____
11. irredeemable _____
12. descend _____
13. community _____
14. interwoven _____
15. antipathy _____

MATCH THE DEFINITION

a. around
b. forward, for
c. self
d. down, away
e. under
f. across
g. over, above
h. together
i. against
j. before
k. middle
l. many
m. between
n. not
o. undo, opposite

ANSWER KEY

PREFIX FINDER

1. f
2. j
3. a
4. k
5. g
6. o
7. l
8. b
9. e
10. c
11. n
12. d
13. h
14. m
15. i

HOW TO PLAY:

Synonyms are words or phrases that mean exactly or nearly the same as another word or phrase. For example, the word "continual" is a synonym for the word "recurring," as both words mean "repeated periodically." But the word "again," which means "once more," would not be a synonym for "continual." In this next game, you must find the word that is *not* a synonym of the others.

SET ONE:

1. Obscure
a. confuse
b. eliminate
c. befuddle
d. hide

2. Emphemeral
a. momentary
b. fleeting
c. perishable
d. brief

3. Remarkable
a. curious
b. unique
c. expensive
d. noteworthy

4. Disgusting
a. foul
b. repellent
c. antagonistic
d. loathsome

ANSWER KEY

SYNONYM PRETENDER

Set One:

1. eliminate
2. perishable
3. expensive
4. antagonistic

HOW TO PLAY:
See instructions on page 71.

SET TWO:

5. Awkward
a. clumsy
b. goofy
c. ungainly
d. uneasy

6. Elevate
a. levitate
b. raise up
c. upgrade
d. erect

7. Barter
a. trade
b. swap
c. take back
d. exchange

8. Distraught
a. grieving
b. troubled
c. worried
d. anxious

ANSWER KEY

SYNONYM PRETENDER

Set Two:

5. goofy

6. upgrade

7. take back

8. grieving

HOW TO PLAY:
See instructions on page 71.

SET THREE:

9. Maximize
a. exaggerate
b. augment
c. lengthen
d. build up

10. Synonym
a. interchangeable
b. equivalent
c. together
d. related

11. Trivial
a. cheap
b. negligible
c. trifling
d. unimportant

12. Conjecture
a. guess
b. challenge
c. speculate
d. suppose

ANSWER KEY

SYNONYM PRETENDER

Set Three:

9. exaggerate

10. together

11. cheap

12. challenge

OXYMORONS

HOW TO PLAY:

An oxymoron is a figure of speech in which two words that contradict each other are used together. An example would be "jumbo shrimp." When we put "jumbo" (large) and "shrimp" (small) together, it opposes common sense, but it is nonetheless an accurate description of a kind of crustacean. An oxymoron is a mini paradox.

In this game, you will connect words from Column A with words from Column B to form common oxymoron phrases.

SET ONE:

COLUMN A	COLUMN B
1. freezer	a. order
2. speed	b. thrift
3. science	c. naturally
4. random	d. history
5. constant	e. despot
6. act	f. burn
7. virtual	g. fiction
8. benevolent	h. change
9. spend	i. limit
10. modern	j. reality

ANSWER KEY

OXYMORONS

Set One:

1. f
2. i
3. g
4. a
5. h
6. c
7. j
8. e
9. b
10. d

HOW TO PLAY:
See instructions on page 77.

SET TWO:
COLUMN A

1. guest
2. crash
3. safety
4. instant
5. pretty
6. civil
7. spectator
8. silent
9. tough
10. opposite

COLUMN B

a. landing
b. war
c. testimony
d. attraction
e. love
f. hazard
g. ugly
h. classic
i. host
j. sport

ANSWER KEY

OXYMORONS

Set Two:

1. i
2. a
3. f
4. h
5. g
6. b
7. j
8. c
9. e
10. d

HOW TO PLAY:

In this game, you must find the two words — one from the first column, one from the second column — that, if combined, could lead to a common expression. For example, the words "ace" and "hole," if combined, could lead to the common expression "ace in the hole." In the first set, time how long it takes you to make all of the matches. Then, in the second set, see if you can beat your time.

SET ONE:

diamond	thumb
pig	sleeve
rough	fly
kite	drop
ointment	wolf
clam	fly
bucket	roll
sheep	rule
poke	happy
nothing	punches

COMMON SAYINGS

Set One:

1. diamond in the rough
2. pig in a poke
3. nothing up my sleeve
4. fly in the ointment
5. drop in the bucket
6. wolf in sheep's clothing
7. go fly a kite
8. roll with the punches
9. rule of thumb
10. happy as a clam

COMMON SAYINGS

HOW TO PLAY:
See instructions on page 81.

SET TWO:

cool	thoughts
sly	golden
spill	stops
picture	flies
penny	hatter
buck	fox
mad	cucumber
time	dam
water	beans
silence	words

ANSWER KEY

COMMON SAYINGS

Set Two:

1. cool as a cucumber
2. sly as a fox
3. don't spill the beans
4. a picture is worth a thousand words
5. penny for your thoughts
6. the buck stops here
7. mad as a hatter
8. time flies
9. water over the dam
10. silence is golden

HOW TO PLAY:

The "hippie" youth movement began in the mid-1960s in the United States and soon spread to countries around the world. Hippies were countercultural pacifists who advocated "making love not war." Often referred to as "flower children," they sometimes lived in communes and were often characterized by long hair, psychedelic rock music, love beads, sexual liberation, and drug use that helped them to achieve altered states of consciousness. They also evolved their own unique and colorful language.

In this exercise, you will be presented with a series of Hippie Terms. Your challenge is to provide the common English definition of each term.

Hippie Terms	Meaning
1. "crash pad"	
2. "What's your bag?"	
3. "Can you dig it?"	
4. "a gas"	
5. "split"	
6. "scene"	
7. "pigs"	
8. "groovy"	
9. "tripping"	
10. "far out"	
11. "selling out"	
12. "threads"	
13. "hang loose"	
14. "flaky"	

Answer Key

HIPPIE LINGO

1. a place to sleep it off
2. What's your thing; what are you into?
3. Do you get it?
4. a blast, a good time
5. leave; depart
6. a happening
7. derogatory term for the police
8. fun, enjoyable
9. having a hallucinogenic experience from drugs
10. taking things to the limit
11. giving in to traditional social-establishment values
12. clothes
13. Take it easy; don't get uptight.
14. ditsy

HOW TO PLAY:

In this game, you will be given half a traditional proverb, with an improbable ending. Your challenge is to guess the correct ending of the proverb.

1. It is always darkest before . . . daylight savings time.

2. Never underestimate the power of . . . nature.

3. It is better to light one small candle . . . than to waste electricity.

4. A rolling stone . . . could crush you.

5. I think, therefore I . . . get a headache.

6. Early to bed and early to rise . . . is the first in the bathroom.

7. A journey of a thousand miles begins with a . . . blister.

8. The grass is always greener . . . when you leave the sprinkler on.

9. Don't count your chickens . . . it takes too long.

10. Where there's smoke there's . . . pollution.

11. A penny saved is . . . a slow road to retirement.

12. Strike while the . . . match is hot.

13. The squeaky wheel . . . gets on your nerves.

14. If you lie down with dogs . . . you'll smell bad when you get up.

15. If you can't stand the heat . . . don't light the fireplace.

ANSWER KEY

TWISTED PROVERBS

1. the dawn
2. human stupidity
3. than to curse the darkness
4. gathers no moss
5. am
6. makes a man healthy, wealthy, and wise
7. single step
8. on the other side
9. before they're hatched
10. fire
11. a penny earned
12. iron is hot
13. gets the oil
14. you'll get up with fleas
15. get out of the kitchen

PART 2:
RIGHT BRAIN

CAN YOU SEE IT?

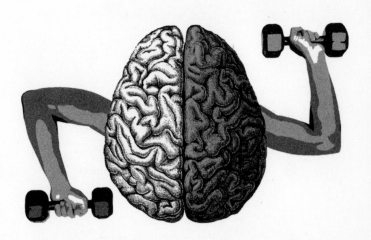

VISUAL PERCEPTION & SPATIAL EXERCISES

RIGHT BRAIN: CAN YOU SEE IT?
VISUAL PERCEPTION & SPATIAL EXERCISES

INTRODUCTION:
The focus of the exercises in this section will be on the right brain's visual-spatial processing strengths. In this workout, your brain will light up as it "sees" the possibilities in the patterns. The puzzles relate to:

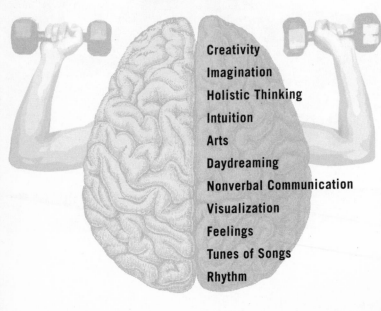

LEFT   RIGHT

Creativity

Imagination

Holistic Thinking

Intuition

Arts

Daydreaming

Nonverbal Communication

Visualization

Feelings

Tunes of Songs

Rhythm

HOW TO PLAY:

In this exercise, you will see two pictures side by side that appear to be exact replicas. But they are not. Your challenge is to identify how the second picture is different from the first.

SET ONE:
BLIND SCHOLAR

Find the five differences between the two images.

ANSWER KEY

COMPARE AND CONTRAST

Set One: Blind Scholar

1. hair lock abutting the left side of the face is missing a black swirl
2. eyes have dash lines
3. right side of nose shading is black not white
4. there is no black shading between nose and mouth
5. missing piece of collar on the right chest

COMPARE AND CONTRAST

HOW TO PLAY:
See instructions on page 91.

SET TWO:
FLORAL PATTERN

Find the five differences between the two images.

ANSWER KEY

COMPARE AND CONTRAST

Set Two: Floral Pattern

1. center swirled stem is turned to the left instead of the right
2. black floral design on the right is missing a petal in the top outer grouping
3. black floral design on the right is missing a set of small, dropping circles at the bottom
4. middle center design has black shading
5. lower left floral grouping has only one outer leaf

Set Three:
Musical Theatre

Find the eight differences between the two images.

ANSWER KEY

COMPARE AND CONTRAST

Set Three: Musical Theatre

1. side accent lines on left mask are pointing to the sides instead of down

2. musical note is missing in the first upper right cluster of notes

3. top ballet slipper is missing lacing cross lines

4. not enough strings on the lowest cord grouping of the violin

5. no accent circle on top of left-side groove of the violin

6. no accent circle on bottom of left-side groove of the violin

7. no accent circle on top of right-side groove of the violin

8. no accent circle on bottom of right-side groove of the violin

HOW TO PLAY:

In the following three sets, you will be presented with four images. All but one of the images appear in the mosaic picture that follows. Your brain challenge is to identify the image that is not part of the collage.

SET ONE:
REINDEER

1

2

3

4

ANSWER KEY

MOSAICS

Set One: Reindeer

Image 2 is not part of the collage.

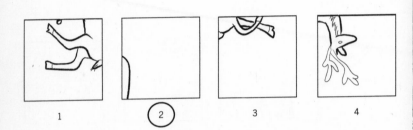

1   2   3   4

HOW TO PLAY:
See instructions on page 97.

SET TWO:
SHARK

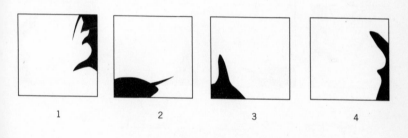

1   2   3   4

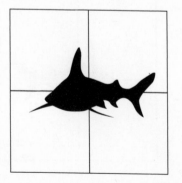

ANSWER KEY

MOSAICS

Set Two: Shark
Image 3 is not part of the collage.

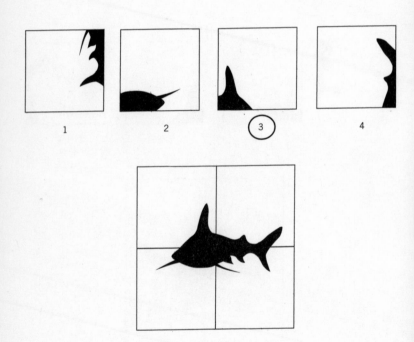

HOW TO PLAY:
See instructions on page 97.

SET THREE:
DANCERS

1

2

3

4

ANSWER KEY

MOSAICS

Set Three: Dancers

Image 4 is not part of the collage.

1

2

3

4

HOW TO PLAY:

In the following three sets of brain teasers, you will see a layered image. Your challenge is to identify the three singular images that must be combined to create the layered image.

SET ONE:
AVIARY

ANSWER KEY

ENTANGLEMENTS

Set One: Aviary

Images 2, 7, and 8 create the layered image at the top.

HOW TO PLAY:
See instructions on page 103.

SET TWO:
WINTER

1

2

3

4

5

6

7

8

9

ANSWER KEY

ENTANGLEMENTS

Set Two: Winter

Images 1, 5, and 9 create the layered image at the top.

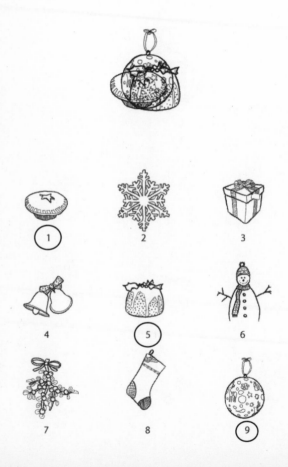

Set Three:
Wardrobe

1

2

3

4

5

6

7

8

9

ANSWER KEY

ENTANGLEMENTS

Set Three: Wardrobe

Images 4, 8, and 9 create the layered image at the top.

1

2

3

4

5

6

7

8

9

HOW TO PLAY:

In each of the following three sets, you will see a group of images. Look at the images. Try to find the image that is different from the rest.

Example: Look at the letters below. Which letter is the odd one out?

C B Q W D

One letter is made with straight lines, while all the others have curved lines. In this example, "W" is the odd one out.

SET ONE:

CORNICES

Which image is the odd one out?

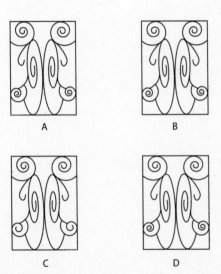

A

B

C

D

ANSWER KEY

ODD ONE OUT

Set One: Cornices

Image C is the odd one out because the bottom curlicues are oversized.

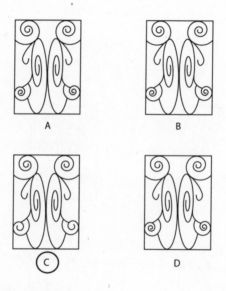

SET TWO:
SCROLLS
Which image doesn't fit the pattern?

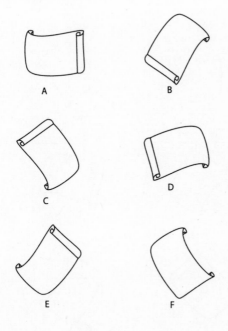

A

B

C

D

E

F

ANSWER KEY

ODD ONE OUT

Set Two: Scrolls

Image F is the odd one out because the curl is inverted.

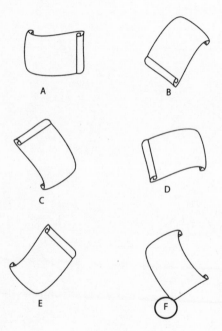

HOW TO PLAY:
See instructions on page 109.

SET THREE:
ALPHABET
What is it about one of the letters of the alphabet below that makes it the odd one out?

A   F

N   W

H

ANSWER KEY

ODD ONE OUT

Set Three: Alphabet

The letter "W" is the odd one out because it is made up of four straight lines, while all the others are made of three lines.

NEXT IN LINE

HOW TO PLAY:

In the next set of exercises, your brain challenge is to identify the object that would logically complete the sequence. The key to the sequence is in the visual pattern. Use your left brain to find the "rule" that orders the pattern, and your right brain to see the visual aspects of the pattern. Use the logic questions to guide you to the correct selection. Choose the correct response from the choices offered.

SET ONE:
STACKED CIRCLES

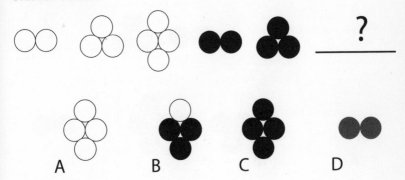

LOGIC QUESTIONS:

1. Consider the question you have to answer: What is the next figure in the sequence?

2. What do you already know about the figures?

3. What do they have in common?

4. What is the relationship among the figures?
   - a. number of sides?
   - b. direction of figures?
   - c. relationship between the figures?
   - d. shading of figures?
   - e. movement of figures?
   - f. combinations of figures?

5. What is the pattern rule?

ANSWER KEY

NEXT IN LINE

Set One: Stacked Circles

The answer is figure C. The black circles should increase by one, just as the white circles do.

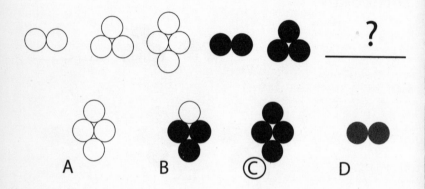

HOW TO PLAY:
See instructions on page 115.

SET TWO:
MOVING STARS

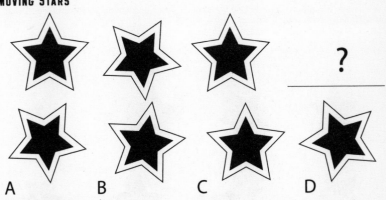

?
_____

A   B   C   D

LOGIC QUESTIONS:

1. Consider the question you have to answer: What is the next figure in the sequence?

2. What do you already know about the figures?

3. What do they have in common?

4. What is the relationship among the figures?
   - a. number of sides?
   - b. direction of figures?
   - c. relationship between the figures?
   - d. shading of figures?
   - e. movement of figures?
   - f. combinations of figures?

5. What is the pattern rule?

ANSWER KEY

NEXT IN LINE

Set Two: Moving Stars

The answer is figure A. The first and third star are the same, so the second and fourth star should match each other.

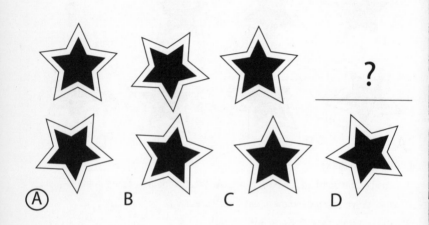

HOW TO PLAY:
See instructions on page 115.

SET THREE:
LIVING SHADOWS

A   B   C   D

LOGIC QUESTIONS:

1. Consider the question you have to answer: What is the next figure in the sequence?

2. What do you know already about the figures?

3. What do they have in common?

4. What is the relationship among the figures?

      a. number of sides?   d. shading of figures?

      b. direction of figures?   e. movement of figures?

      c. relationship between the figures?   f. combinations of figures?

5. What is the pattern rule?

ANSWER KEY

NEXT IN LINE

Set Three: Living Shadows

The answer is figure B because the repeating pattern is fish, mammal, bird.

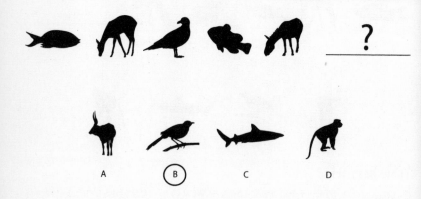

A   B   C   D

How to Play:
See instructions on page 115.

Set Four:
Snowflakes

A   B   C   D

Logic Questions:

1. Consider the question you have to answer: What is the next figure in the sequence?

2. What do you know already about the figures?

3. What do they have in common?

4. What is the relationship among the figures?
   - a. number of sides?
   - b. direction of figures?
   - c. relationship between the figures?
   - d. shading of figures?
   - e. movement of figures?
   - f. combinations of figures?

5. What is the pattern rule?

ANSWER KEY

NEXT IN LINE

Set Four: Snowflakes

The answer is figure C. The first three figures are different, but they all have three stems at the top; the pattern for the next three figures is that each repeats the first sequence, but this time they all have two stems (not three) at the top.

How to Play:
See instructions on page 115.

Set Five:
Arrow Rotations

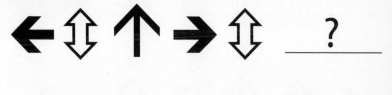

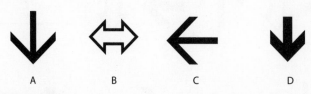

A   B   C   D

Logic Questions:

1. Consider the question you have to answer: What is the next figure in the sequence?

2. What do you know already about the figures?

3. What do they have in common?

4. What is the relationship among the figures?
   - a. number of sides?
   - b. direction of figures?
   - c. relationship between the figures?
   - d. shading of figures?
   - e. movement of figures?
   - f. combinations of figures?

5. What is the pattern rule?

ANSWER KEY

NEXT IN LINE

Set Five: Arrow Rotations

The answer is figure A. The pattern is bold arrow pointing left, white arrow pointing up and down, thin arrow pointing up; then, bold arrow pointing right, white arrow pointing up and down, and thin arrow pointing down.

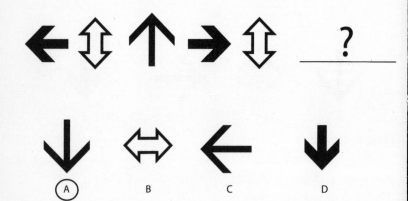

HOW TO PLAY:

The following two sets involve both memory and visual perception. For each set, you will be presented with two grids. One grid will have a graphic design superimposed on it. The other grid is blank. Your brain challenge is to reproduce the design on the left by drawing every element of it in the same location on the blank grid on the right.

SET ONE:
CROSSOVERS

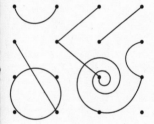

ANSWER KEY

COPYCAT

Set One: Crossovers

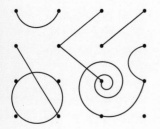 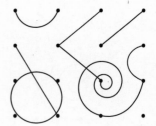

How to Play:
See instructions on page 125.

Set Two:
Twirls and Swirls

ANSWER KEY

COPYCAT

Set Two: Twirls and Swirls

HOW TO PLAY:

In this brain challenge, you will be presented with two optical illusions. Optical illusions play tricks with the way your brain receives visual stimuli. For each illusion, a question will be posed. Answering the question will help you see your way toward solving the illusion.

SET ONE:

TWO-HEADED CRITTER

There are two critters in this illusion . . . one lives on land, and the other in the water. What are they?

ANSWER KEY

OPTICAL ILLUSIONS

Set One: Two-Headed Critter

The two critters are a duck and a rabbit.

HOW TO PLAY:

See instructions on page 129.

SET TWO:

MIRROR IMAGES

The foreground and background are reversible in this illusion, creating two distinct pictures. What two images do you see?

ANSWER KEY

OPTICAL ILLUSIONS

Set Two: Mirror Images

The images are a vase in white and two faces in black.

How to Play:

Use your right brain to see your way through the following four mazes. Trace an unobstructed path through each maze, beginning at the "Start" and ending at the "Finish."

Set One:
Roaring Lion

ANSWER KEY

MAZE HAZE

Set One: Roaring Lion

START

FINISH

Set Two:
Interlocking Circles

MAZE HAZE

Set Two: Interlocking Circles

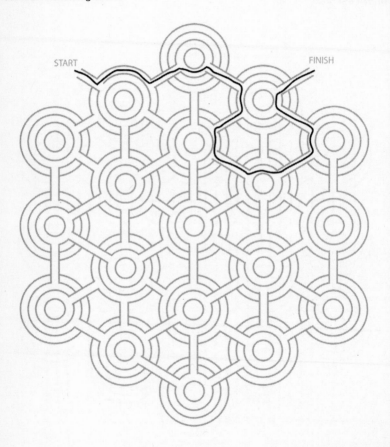

MAZE HAZE

HOW TO PLAY:
See instructions on page 133.

SET THREE:
SQUARE STUFF

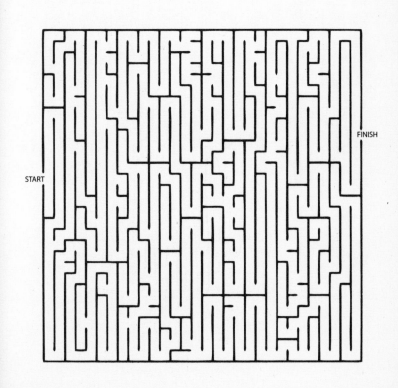

START

FINISH

ANSWER KEY

MAZE HAZE

Set Three: Square Stuff

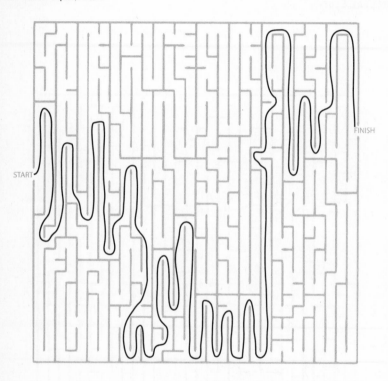

START

FINISH

How to Play:
See instructions on page 133.

Set Four:
Fireball

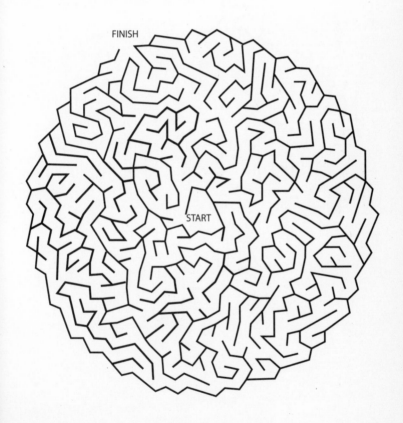

ANSWER KEY

MAZE HAZE

Set Four: Fireball

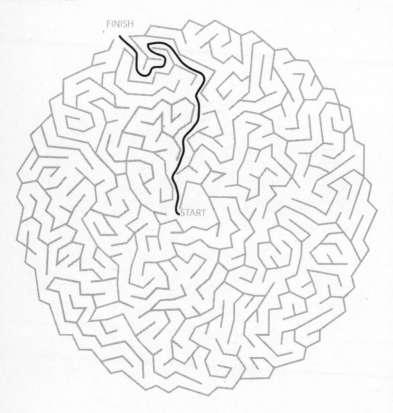

FINISH

START

PART 3:
WHOLE BRAIN

CAN YOU THINK IT?

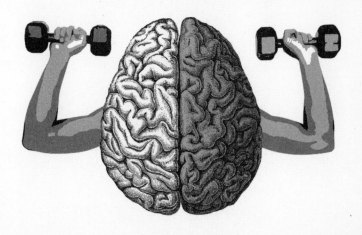

WHOLE BRAIN: CAN YOU THINK IT?
INTUITIVE-THINKING EXERCISES

INTRODUCTION:
The focus of the exercises in this section is on whole-brain thinking. In this workout, you'll draw on your left brain's analytical processes and your right brain's creative-intuitive processes to solve the puzzles using "out of the box" thinking.

LEFT   RIGHT

LEFT	RIGHT
Logic	Creativity
Analysis	Imagination
Sequencing	Holistic Thinking
Linear Reasoning	Intuition
Mathematics	Arts
Language	Rhythm
Facts	Nonverbal Communication
Thinking in Words	Visualization
Words of Songs	Feelings
Computation	Tunes of Songs
	Daydreaming

How to Play:

AHA! puzzles are those frustrating and challenging puzzles with answers that seem "obvious" — *after* you solve them. However, in order to get to the obvious answer, your brain needs to do some complex parallel processing that synthesizes input from both the left- and right-brain hemispheres. Solving AHA! puzzles requires creative thinking, and the answers often come in a flash of awareness. You cannot simply "think" the solutions to these puzzles in a traditional sense. Rather, you will need to draw on both logic and visual perception.

Set One:

Parlez-Vous Français?

You are at a garden party hosted by the Count and Countess de Vine at Le Chateau Bordeaux. Go on, don't be shy. Even though you may not speak French very well, raise a glass and try to make some kind of "chat."

ANSWER KEY

AHA! PUZZLES

Set One: Parlez-Vous Français?

In French, the word "chat" means cat, so just raise the glass in the picture to create this cat face.

How to Play:
See instructions on page 143.

Set Two:

Suited Up

As you can see, Biscuit the Clown is wearing a very snazzy suit. His favorite party trick is to change out of it into another suit at the drop of a hat. What does this other suit look like?

ANSWER KEY

AHA! PUZZLES

Set Two: Suited Up

Drop the hat to the bottom of the picture, color Biscuit's suit black, and you have the representation of the card suit — spades.

Set Three:
Ruffled Feathers

What feathered creature do you see?

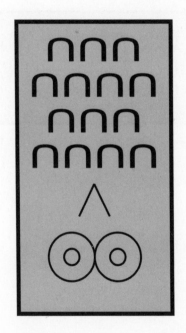

AHA! PUZZLES

Set Three: Ruffled Feathers

Rotate the original image, and you will see an owl on its side.

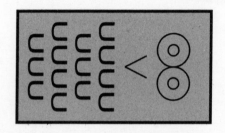

HOW TO PLAY:

You will be presented with six sets of words. The words in each set provide clues to a hobby. Your challenge is to use the clue words to guess the hobby for each set.

Set One
aperture
cropping
exposure
negative

Set Two
bind off
purl
cast on
needle

Set Three
cleat
dead ahead
stern
wake

Set Four
belay
edging
bouldering
rappel

Set Five
bonk
bunny hop
chain suck
downshift

Set Six
back tack
baste marking
notches
sizing

ANSWER KEY

WHAT'S MY HOBBY?

Set One: photography

Set Two: knitting

Set Three: boating

Set Four: mountain climbing

Set Five: cycling

Set Six: sewing

HOW TO PLAY:

In the following 16 sets, you will be presented with lists containing three items each. One of the items does not belong in the list, because it differs in some fundamental way from the remaining two items. Your job is to find and circle the "odd one out" in each set. Here's an example:

Maltese, poodle, spaniel

While all of these are dogs, you would circle spaniel. Do you know why? That's right — a spaniel has dog fur, while the other two breeds have nonallergenic "real" hair.

Set One
Siamese
Maltese
Bernese

Set Two
Memorial Day
Labor Day
Halloween

Set Three
cirrus
sedimentary
cumulonimbus

Set Four
furnace
volcano
teapot

ANSWER KEY

TAKE IT AWAY

Set One: Siamese (Maltese and Bernese are dogs.)

Set Two: Halloween (Memorial Day and Labor Day are national holidays.)

Set Three: sedimentary (Cirrus and cumulonimbus are types of clouds.)

Set Four: furnace (A volcano and a teapot "blow their tops.")

Set Five
doorbell
door knocker
doorknob

Set Six
rickshaw
bicycle
car

Set Seven
frigid
tepid
scorching

Set Eight
John Quincy Adams
Franklin D. Roosevelt
George W. Bush

ANSWER KEY

TAKE IT AWAY

Set Five: doorknob (A doorbell and a door knocker make a sound.)

Set Six: car (A rickshaw and a bicycle have two wheels.)

Set Seven: frigid (Tepid and scorching are degrees of warmth.)

Set Eight: Franklin D. Roosevelt (John Quincy Adams and George W. Bush had fathers who were presidents, too.)

HOW TO PLAY:
See instructions on page 151.

Set Nine
gallon
pint
ton

Set Ten
Milky Way
Orion
Big Dipper

Set Eleven
mambo
Lindy Hop
tango

Set Twelve
Rocky Mountain spotted fever
ALS
Lyme disease

ANSWER KEY

TAKE IT AWAY

Set Nine: ton (A gallon and a pint measure volume.)

Set Ten: Milky Way (The Milky Way is a galaxy; Orion and the Big Dipper are star constellations.)

Set Eleven: Lindy Hop (The mambo and the tango are Latin styles of dance.)

Set Twelve: ALS (Rocky Mountain spotted fever and Lyme disease are tick-borne diseases.)

Set Thirteen
Raisinettes
Three Musketeers
Snickers

Set Fourteen
mah-jongg
canasta
bridge

Set Fifteen
basketball
baseball
tennis

Set Sixteen
Mercedes
Honda
Porsche

Answer Key

Set Thirteen: Snickers (Raisinettes and Three Musketeers candies don't have nuts.)

Set Fourteen: mah-jongg (Mah-jongg uses tiles; canasta and bridge are card games.)

Set Fifteen: baseball (Basketball and tennis are played with nets.)

Set Sixteen: Honda (The Mercedes and Porsche are high-priced vehicles.)

HOW TO PLAY:

In this game, you will be presented with 15 sets of five clues each. The sets of clues represent characteristics of an object or a type of person. You must put the clues together to identify the person or thing each set describes.

Here is an example:

Clues: *short, green, blade, roots, yard*
Answer: *grass*

Set One
spouse
summons
custody
judge
court

Set Two
small
swallow
daily
health
C, D, E

Set Three
stone
inherit
royal
cold
edifice

Answer:

Answer:

Answer:

ANSWER KEY

WHAT AM I?

Set One: divorce
Set Two: vitamin
Set Three: castle

HOW TO PLAY:

See instructions on page 159.

Set Four
football
rollerblading
head
motorcycle
hard

Answer:

Set Five
bowl
spiked
liquid
recipe
celebrate

Answer:

Set Six
months
numbers
appointments
holidays
calendar

Answer:

ANSWER KEY

WHAT AM I?

Set Four: helmet
Set Five: punch
Set Six: datebook

HOW TO PLAY:
See instructions on page 159.

Set Seven
elastic
lenses
vision
protection
waterproof

Answer:

Set Eight
experience
typed
paper
network
interview

Answer:

Set Nine
blade
binding
poles
feet
mountain

Answer:

ANSWER KEY

WHAT AM I?

Set Seven: goggles

Set Eight: resume

Set Nine: skis

How to Play:

See instructions on page 159.

Set Ten
sticks
carrot
coal
ball
cold

Answer:

Set Eleven
track
cars
tickets
scenic
travel

Answer:

Set Twelve
patch
orange
fall
farmer
pie

Answer:

Set Thirteen
stars
birthdays
prophecy
future
signs

Answer:

Set Fourteen
connected
browser
search
friends
social

Answer:

Set Fifteen
identification
letters
numbers
states
vehicle

Answer:

ANSWER KEY

WHAT AM I?

Set Ten: snowman

Set Eleven: train

Set Twelve: pumpkin

Set Thirteen: horoscope

Set Fourteen: Facebook

Set Fifteen: license plate

How to Play:

A "rebus" is a pictorial representation of a name, word, or common phrase. To solve the following seven sets of rebus puzzles, you must combine your visual and verbal perceptions to lead you to a creative answer. The example below illustrates how the thought process works. In this example, the word "head" is placed over the word "heels." The black line represents the over/under relationship. Put the visual and verbal clues together and you get the common expression below.

HEAD
—————— = *HEAD OVER HEELS*
HEELS

Set One:

LOOKING TIRED

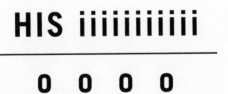

ANSWER KEY

REBUS RIDDLES

Set One: Looking Tired
circles under his eyes

SET TWO:

GIVE AWAY

Grab

Grab

Grab

Grab

REBUS RIDDLES

Set Two: Give Away
up for grabs

HOW TO PLAY:
See instructions on page 167.

SET THREE:
CITY PLACE

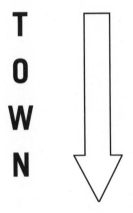

ANSWER KEY

REBUS RIDDLES

Set Three: City Place

downtown

HOW TO PLAY:
See instructions on page 167.

SET FOUR:
EMBARRASSED

F A r e d C E

ANSWER KEY

REBUS RIDDLES

Set Four: Embarrassed

red in the face

HOW TO PLAY:
See instructions on page 167.

SET FIVE:

UNDER THE WEATHER

B s i c k E D

ANSWER KEY

REBUS RIDDLES

Set Five: Under the Weather

sick in bed

HOW TO PLAY:
See instructions on page 167.

SET SIX:
EYESTRAIN

R/E/A/D/I/N/G

REBUS RIDDLES

Set Six: Eyestrain
reading between the lines

HOW TO PLAY:
See instructions on page 167.

SET SEVEN:

TRAVEL PLANS

TRAVEL

CCCCCC

ANSWER KEY

REBUS RIDDLES

Set Seven: Travel Plans

overseas travel

HOW TO PLAY:

Figure out the relationship among the items in the sequence. Then identify the item that would come next in the sequence. Look at the example below.

say, you, by, dawn's, light _____

The last word to complete the sequence is "so." Do you know why? That's right. The words represent the opening lyrics from "The Star-Spangled Banner," with every other word missing from the lyrics.

1. b, f, j, n, r, _____

2. elephant, camel, lion, dog, _____

3. u, o, i, e, _____

4. diamond, emerald, pearl, ruby, peridot, _____

5. ace, eight, five, four, jack, _____

6. Alabama, Alaska, California, Colorado, Delaware, Florida, Georgia, _____

7. kindergarten, middle school, high school, bachelor, master's, _____

8. bronze, silver, gold, _____

9. aqua, crimson, emerald, green, _____

10. Biden, Cheney, Gore, Quayle, _____

11. 46, 40, 39, 33, 32, 26, _____

12. love, 15, 30, 40, _____

13. frog, tadpole, _____

14. J, O, P, Q, R, _____

15. double bogey, bogey, par, _____

ANSWER KEY

SEQUENCE SOLVER

1. v (increase by 4 letters)
2. any mammal smaller a than dog (decreasing by size)
3. a (vowels in reverse order)
4. sapphire (birthstones, in order of months)
5. king (playing cards, by first-letter alphabetical order)
6. Hawaii (U.S. states in alphabetical order, by first letter of state)
7. Ph.D. (advancing academic degrees)
8. platinum (metals by increasing industrial worth)
9. ivory or indigo (names of colors in alphabetical order, skipping every other letter)
10. Bush (vice presidents in reverse order)
11. 25 (pattern is subtract by 6, subtract by 1, and repeat)
12. game (tennis points, with scores in increasing value)
13. egg (life cycle of a frog in reverse order)
14. S (increasing capital letters of the alphabet that are formed using rounded lines)
15. birdie (golf scores per hole, by decreasing number of strokes)

HOW TO PLAY:

In the following exercise, each group of numbers and letters combines to form a familiar statement. See how quickly you can find the solution to the word formula. For example:

Word Formula: 5 = N. of P. on a B. T.

Solution: 5 = number of players on a basketball team

a. 12 = E. in a D.

b. 52 = W. in a Y.

c. 5 = F. on a H.

d. 4 = Q. in a D.

e. 26 = L. in the A.

f. 8 = P. in the S. S.

g. 52 = P.C. in a D.

h. 8 = O. in a C.

ANSWER KEY

WORD FORMULAS

a. eggs in a dozen

b. weeks in a year

c. fingers on a hand

d. quarters in a dollar

e. letters in the alphabet

f. planets in the solar system

g. playing cards in a deck

h. ounces in a cup

How to Play:

A "palindrome" is a word, phrase, verse, or sentence that reads the same backward or forward. In this game, you will be given a clue for a one-word palindrome. Your challenge is to use the clue to identify the palindrome, as in the example below.

Clue: A call for help.

Answer: SOS

1. an explosive device

2. a baby barnyard-animal sound

3. Adam's significant other

4. male and female genders

5. a sound made by a train

6. a small child

7. the opposite of "bro"

8. an expression of surprise or delight

9. Mario Andretti drives one

10. what you look through

11. a type of boat for rowing on water

12. how you address a married Frenchwoman

13. midday

14. a type of rally held before a school sporting event, like football or basketball

15. a female sheep

ANSWER KEY

PALINDROMES

1. TNT
2. peep
3. Eve
4. sexes
5. toot
6. tot
7. sis
8. wow
9. race car
10. eye
11. kayak
12. madam
13. noon
14. pep
15. ewe

MINI MYSTERIES

HOW TO PLAY:

Each of the sets of riddles that follow contains a concealed truth. Solve the riddle and find the truth. Riddles are not difficult to solve if you use your imagination and trust your intuition. Often the truths hidden in riddles are quite simple and just require a little "out of the box" thinking.

SET ONE:

1. Elizabeth is taking a class at a local community college in her spare time. She's given a vocabulary sheet full of terms like "meter," "time," "3/4", "clef," and "scale." What is she learning about?

2. Little Jolee goes to visit Grandma in Florida. When she gets home her Mom asks her what she did with Grandma. Jolee says they walked around strangers' lawns looking for old toys. What were Jolee and Grandma doing?

3. Dan is looking for milk in the refrigerator. He sees milk in a plastic container, but he doesn't drink it. He tells his wife that they are out of milk. She comes into the kitchen carrying the baby. She looks in the refrigerator and agrees that they are out of milk. She says she'll pick some up today. How is this possible?

ANSWER KEY

MINI MYSTERIES

Set One:

1. music theory

2. They were going to yard sales.

3. The refrigerated milk is breast milk for the baby.

MINI MYSTERIES

HOW TO PLAY:
See instructions on page 187.

SET TWO:

1. Sophie and Mike share a house, but they each have their own families and never see each other inside their house. How is this possible?

2. Jim is considered a champion at his job. He always wears gloves when working, but his hands are often sore and bruised despite the gloves. Sometimes he even injures his coworkers on purpose. What is Jim's job?

3. Coleen is distracted from her work by a loud howling noise coming from outside her window. She goes to investigate. The second she steps outside, she knows what the noise is. However, she cannot see what is making the noise, she can only feel it. What is the noise?

ANSWER KEY

MINI MYSTERIES

Set Two:

1. They live in a two-family house.

2. boxer

3. the wind

I want to thank the following people who made this book possible — from Sellers Publishing: Publishing Director Robin Haywood; Editor in Chief, Books, Mark Chimsky; Managing Editor Mary Baldwin; and Production Editor Charlotte Cromwell; as well as proofreader Renee Rooks Cooley; book designer George Corsillo, Design Monsters; designer Bill Becker, BC Graphics; my agent, Coleen O'Shea, Allen O'Shea Literary Agency; and Dr. Francis M. Crinella, neuropsychology contributor. I would also like to thank my friends and family for their continued support and encouragement.

— *Corinne L. Gediman*